THIS *journal* BELONGS TO:

A

WEBSITE
USERNAME
PASSWORD
PIN/HINT
OTHER

WEBSITE
USERNAME
PASSWORD
PIN/HINT
OTHER

WEBSITE
USERNAME
PASSWORD
PIN/HINT
OTHER

WEBSITE
USERNAME
PASSWORD
PIN/HINT
OTHER

A

WEBSITE	
USERNAME	
PASSWORD	
PIN/HINT	
OTHER	

WEBSITE	
USERNAME	
PASSWORD	
PIN/HINT	
OTHER	

WEBSITE	
USERNAME	
PASSWORD	
PIN/HINT	
OTHER	

WEBSITE	
USERNAME	
PASSWORD	
PIN/HINT	
OTHER	

A

WEBSITE	
USERNAME	
PASSWORD	
PIN/HINT	
OTHER	

WEBSITE	
USERNAME	
PASSWORD	
PIN/HINT	
OTHER	

WEBSITE	
USERNAME	
PASSWORD	
PIN/HINT	
OTHER	

WEBSITE	
USERNAME	
PASSWORD	
PIN/HINT	
OTHER	

A

WEBSITE	
USERNAME	
PASSWORD	
PIN/HINT	
OTHER	

WEBSITE	
USERNAME	
PASSWORD	
PIN/HINT	
OTHER	

WEBSITE	
USERNAME	
PASSWORD	
PIN/HINT	
OTHER	

WEBSITE	
USERNAME	
PASSWORD	
PIN/HINT	
OTHER	

B

WEBSITE
USERNAME
PASSWORD
PIN/HINT
OTHER

WEBSITE
USERNAME
PASSWORD
PIN/HINT
OTHER

WEBSITE
USERNAME
PASSWORD
PIN/HINT
OTHER

WEBSITE
USERNAME
PASSWORD
PIN/HINT
OTHER

WEBSITE	
USERNAME	
PASSWORD	
PIN/HINT	
OTHER	

WEBSITE	
USERNAME	
PASSWORD	
PIN/HINT	
OTHER	

WEBSITE	
USERNAME	
PASSWORD	
PIN/HINT	
OTHER	

WEBSITE	
USERNAME	
PASSWORD	
PIN/HINT	
OTHER	

B

WEBSITE
USERNAME
PASSWORD
PIN/HINT
OTHER

WEBSITE
USERNAME
PASSWORD
PIN/HINT
OTHER

WEBSITE
USERNAME
PASSWORD
PIN/HINT
OTHER

WEBSITE
USERNAME
PASSWORD
PIN/HINT
OTHER

B

WEBSITE
USERNAME
PASSWORD
PIN/HINT
OTHER

WEBSITE
USERNAME
PASSWORD
PIN/HINT
OTHER

WEBSITE
USERNAME
PASSWORD
PIN/HINT
OTHER

WEBSITE
USERNAME
PASSWORD
PIN/HINT
OTHER

C

WEBSITE
USERNAME
PASSWORD
PIN/HINT
OTHER

WEBSITE
USERNAME
PASSWORD
PIN/HINT
OTHER

WEBSITE
USERNAME
PASSWORD
PIN/HINT
OTHER

WEBSITE
USERNAME
PASSWORD
PIN/HINT
OTHER

C

WEBSITE	
USERNAME	
PASSWORD	
PIN/HINT	
OTHER	

WEBSITE	
USERNAME	
PASSWORD	
PIN/HINT	
OTHER	

WEBSITE	
USERNAME	
PASSWORD	
PIN/HINT	
OTHER	

WEBSITE	
USERNAME	
PASSWORD	
PIN/HINT	
OTHER	

C

WEBSITE
USERNAME
PASSWORD
PIN/HINT
OTHER

WEBSITE
USERNAME
PASSWORD
PIN/HINT
OTHER

WEBSITE
USERNAME
PASSWORD
PIN/HINT
OTHER

WEBSITE
USERNAME
PASSWORD
PIN/HINT
OTHER

C

WEBSITE
USERNAME
PASSWORD
PIN/HINT
OTHER

WEBSITE
USERNAME
PASSWORD
PIN/HINT
OTHER

WEBSITE
USERNAME
PASSWORD
PIN/HINT
OTHER

WEBSITE
USERNAME
PASSWORD
PIN/HINT
OTHER

D

WEBSITE
USERNAME
PASSWORD
PIN/HINT
OTHER

WEBSITE
USERNAME
PASSWORD
PIN/HINT
OTHER

WEBSITE
USERNAME
PASSWORD
PIN/HINT
OTHER

WEBSITE
USERNAME
PASSWORD
PIN/HINT
OTHER

D

WEBSITE	
USERNAME	
PASSWORD	
PIN/HINT	
OTHER	

WEBSITE	
USERNAME	
PASSWORD	
PIN/HINT	
OTHER	

WEBSITE	
USERNAME	
PASSWORD	
PIN/HINT	
OTHER	

WEBSITE	
USERNAME	
PASSWORD	
PIN/HINT	
OTHER	

D

WEBSITE
USERNAME
PASSWORD
PIN/HINT
OTHER

WEBSITE
USERNAME
PASSWORD
PIN/HINT
OTHER

WEBSITE
USERNAME
PASSWORD
PIN/HINT
OTHER

WEBSITE
USERNAME
PASSWORD
PIN/HINT
OTHER

D

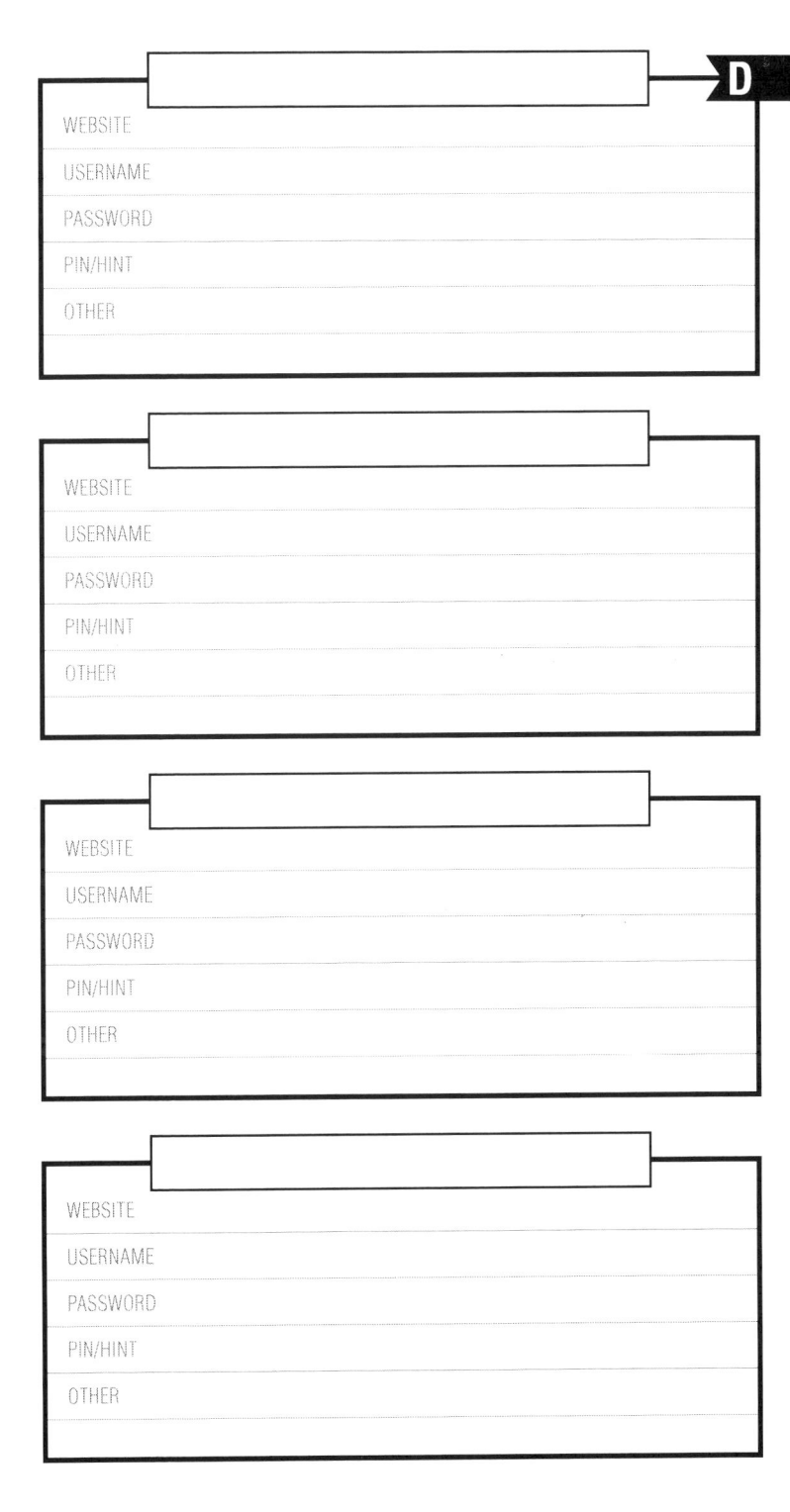

WEBSITE
USERNAME
PASSWORD
PIN/HINT
OTHER

WEBSITE
USERNAME
PASSWORD
PIN/HINT
OTHER

WEBSITE
USERNAME
PASSWORD
PIN/HINT
OTHER

WEBSITE
USERNAME
PASSWORD
PIN/HINT
OTHER

E

WEBSITE
USERNAME
PASSWORD
PIN/HINT
OTHER

WEBSITE
USERNAME
PASSWORD
PIN/HINT
OTHER

WEBSITE
USERNAME
PASSWORD
PIN/HINT
OTHER

WEBSITE
USERNAME
PASSWORD
PIN/HINT
OTHER

E

WEBSITE
USERNAME
PASSWORD
PIN/HINT
OTHER

WEBSITE
USERNAME
PASSWORD
PIN/HINT
OTHER

WEBSITE
USERNAME
PASSWORD
PIN/HINT
OTHER

WEBSITE
USERNAME
PASSWORD
PIN/HINT
OTHER

E

WEBSITE
USERNAME
PASSWORD
PIN/HINT
OTHER

WEBSITE
USERNAME
PASSWORD
PIN/HINT
OTHER

WEBSITE
USERNAME
PASSWORD
PIN/HINT
OTHER

WEBSITE
USERNAME
PASSWORD
PIN/HINT
OTHER

E

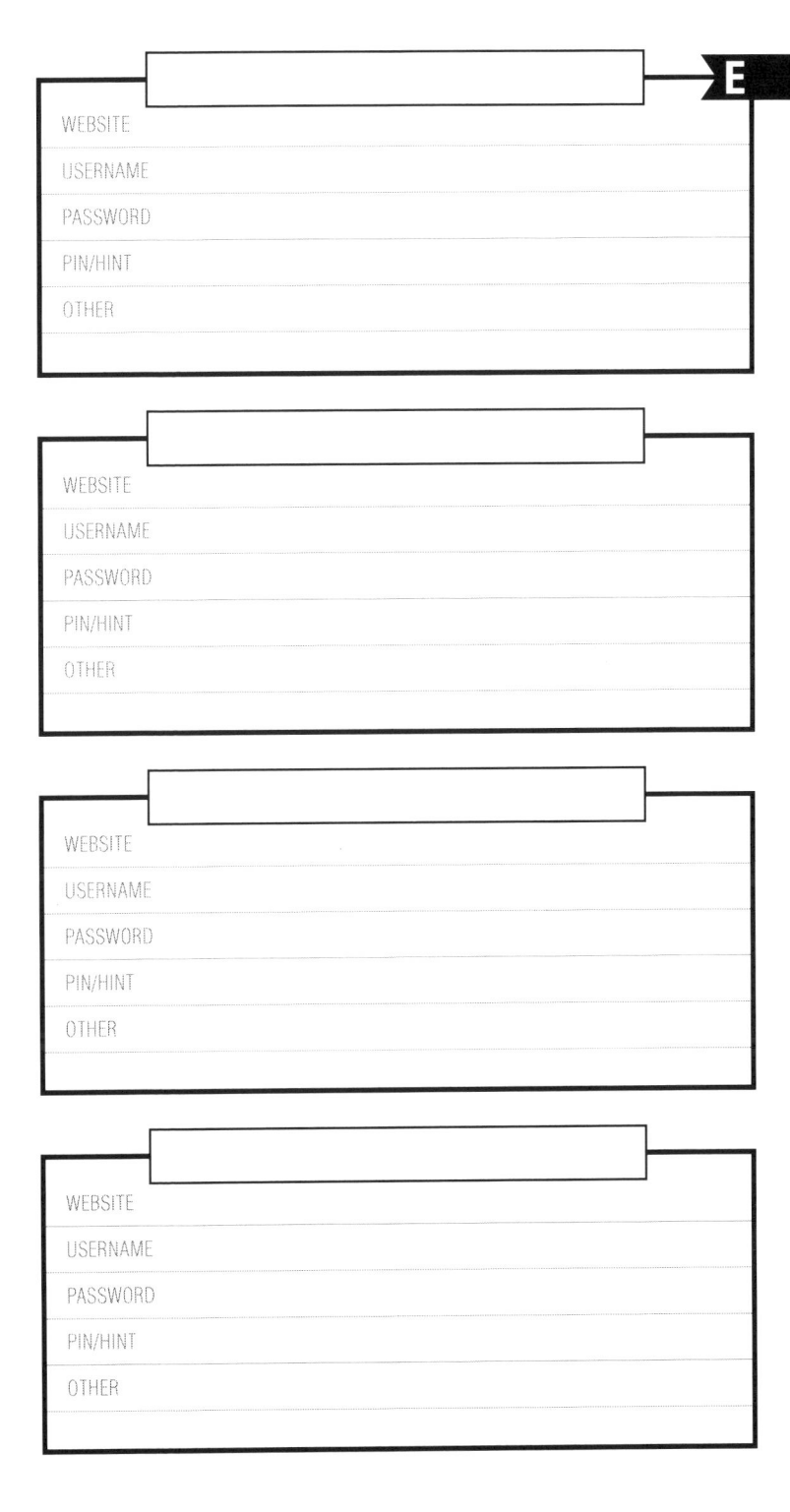

WEBSITE
USERNAME
PASSWORD
PIN/HINT
OTHER

WEBSITE
USERNAME
PASSWORD
PIN/HINT
OTHER

WEBSITE
USERNAME
PASSWORD
PIN/HINT
OTHER

WEBSITE
USERNAME
PASSWORD
PIN/HINT
OTHER

F

WEBSITE
USERNAME
PASSWORD
PIN/HINT
OTHER

WEBSITE
USERNAME
PASSWORD
PIN/HINT
OTHER

WEBSITE
USERNAME
PASSWORD
PIN/HINT
OTHER

WEBSITE
USERNAME
PASSWORD
PIN/HINT
OTHER

F

WEBSITE	
USERNAME	
PASSWORD	
PIN/HINT	
OTHER	

WEBSITE	
USERNAME	
PASSWORD	
PIN/HINT	
OTHER	

WEBSITE	
USERNAME	
PASSWORD	
PIN/HINT	
OTHER	

WEBSITE	
USERNAME	
PASSWORD	
PIN/HINT	
OTHER	

F

WEBSITE
USERNAME
PASSWORD
PIN/HINT
OTHER

WEBSITE
USERNAME
PASSWORD
PIN/HINT
OTHER

WEBSITE
USERNAME
PASSWORD
PIN/HINT
OTHER

WEBSITE
USERNAME
PASSWORD
PIN/HINT
OTHER

F

WEBSITE	
USERNAME	
PASSWORD	
PIN/HINT	
OTHER	

WEBSITE	
USERNAME	
PASSWORD	
PIN/HINT	
OTHER	

WEBSITE	
USERNAME	
PASSWORD	
PIN/HINT	
OTHER	

WEBSITE	
USERNAME	
PASSWORD	
PIN/HINT	
OTHER	

G

WEBSITE	
USERNAME	
PASSWORD	
PIN/HINT	
OTHER	

WEBSITE	
USERNAME	
PASSWORD	
PIN/HINT	
OTHER	

WEBSITE	
USERNAME	
PASSWORD	
PIN/HINT	
OTHER	

WEBSITE	
USERNAME	
PASSWORD	
PIN/HINT	
OTHER	

G

WEBSITE	
USERNAME	
PASSWORD	
PIN/HINT	
OTHER	

WEBSITE	
USERNAME	
PASSWORD	
PIN/HINT	
OTHER	

WEBSITE	
USERNAME	
PASSWORD	
PIN/HINT	
OTHER	

WEBSITE	
USERNAME	
PASSWORD	
PIN/HINT	
OTHER	

G

WEBSITE
USERNAME
PASSWORD
PIN/HINT
OTHER

WEBSITE
USERNAME
PASSWORD
PIN/HINT
OTHER

WEBSITE
USERNAME
PASSWORD
PIN/HINT
OTHER

WEBSITE
USERNAME
PASSWORD
PIN/HINT
OTHER

G

WEBSITE
USERNAME
PASSWORD
PIN/HINT
OTHER

WEBSITE
USERNAME
PASSWORD
PIN/HINT
OTHER

WEBSITE
USERNAME
PASSWORD
PIN/HINT
OTHER

WEBSITE
USERNAME
PASSWORD
PIN/HINT
OTHER

H

WEBSITE
USERNAME
PASSWORD
PIN/HINT
OTHER

WEBSITE
USERNAME
PASSWORD
PIN/HINT
OTHER

WEBSITE
USERNAME
PASSWORD
PIN/HINT
OTHER

WEBSITE
USERNAME
PASSWORD
PIN/HINT
OTHER

H

WEBSITE
USERNAME
PASSWORD
PIN/HINT
OTHER

WEBSITE
USERNAME
PASSWORD
PIN/HINT
OTHER

WEBSITE
USERNAME
PASSWORD
PIN/HINT
OTHER

WEBSITE
USERNAME
PASSWORD
PIN/HINT
OTHER

H

WEBSITE
USERNAME
PASSWORD
PIN/HINT
OTHER

WEBSITE
USERNAME
PASSWORD
PIN/HINT
OTHER

WEBSITE
USERNAME
PASSWORD
PIN/HINT
OTHER

WEBSITE
USERNAME
PASSWORD
PIN/HINT
OTHER

H

WEBSITE
USERNAME
PASSWORD
PIN/HINT
OTHER

WEBSITE
USERNAME
PASSWORD
PIN/HINT
OTHER

WEBSITE
USERNAME
PASSWORD
PIN/HINT
OTHER

WEBSITE
USERNAME
PASSWORD
PIN/HINT
OTHER

I

WEBSITE	
USERNAME	
PASSWORD	
PIN/HINT	
OTHER	

WEBSITE	
USERNAME	
PASSWORD	
PIN/HINT	
OTHER	

WEBSITE	
USERNAME	
PASSWORD	
PIN/HINT	
OTHER	

WEBSITE	
USERNAME	
PASSWORD	
PIN/HINT	
OTHER	

WEBSITE	
USERNAME	
PASSWORD	
PIN/HINT	
OTHER	

WEBSITE	
USERNAME	
PASSWORD	
PIN/HINT	
OTHER	

WEBSITE	
USERNAME	
PASSWORD	
PIN/HINT	
OTHER	

WEBSITE	
USERNAME	
PASSWORD	
PIN/HINT	
OTHER	

I

WEBSITE	
USERNAME	
PASSWORD	
PIN/HINT	
OTHER	

WEBSITE	
USERNAME	
PASSWORD	
PIN/HINT	
OTHER	

WEBSITE	
USERNAME	
PASSWORD	
PIN/HINT	
OTHER	

WEBSITE	
USERNAME	
PASSWORD	
PIN/HINT	
OTHER	

WEBSITE
USERNAME
PASSWORD
PIN/HINT
OTHER

WEBSITE
USERNAME
PASSWORD
PIN/HINT
OTHER

WEBSITE
USERNAME
PASSWORD
PIN/HINT
OTHER

WEBSITE
USERNAME
PASSWORD
PIN/HINT
OTHER

J

WEBSITE
USERNAME
PASSWORD
PIN/HINT
OTHER

WEBSITE
USERNAME
PASSWORD
PIN/HINT
OTHER

WEBSITE
USERNAME
PASSWORD
PIN/HINT
OTHER

WEBSITE
USERNAME
PASSWORD
PIN/HINT
OTHER

J

WEBSITE	
USERNAME	
PASSWORD	
PIN/HINT	
OTHER	

WEBSITE	
USERNAME	
PASSWORD	
PIN/HINT	
OTHER	

WEBSITE	
USERNAME	
PASSWORD	
PIN/HINT	
OTHER	

WEBSITE	
USERNAME	
PASSWORD	
PIN/HINT	
OTHER	

J

WEBSITE
USERNAME
PASSWORD
PIN/HINT
OTHER

WEBSITE
USERNAME
PASSWORD
PIN/HINT
OTHER

WEBSITE
USERNAME
PASSWORD
PIN/HINT
OTHER

WEBSITE
USERNAME
PASSWORD
PIN/HINT
OTHER

J

WEBSITE
USERNAME
PASSWORD
PIN/HINT
OTHER

WEBSITE
USERNAME
PASSWORD
PIN/HINT
OTHER

WEBSITE
USERNAME
PASSWORD
PIN/HINT
OTHER

WEBSITE
USERNAME
PASSWORD
PIN/HINT
OTHER

K

WEBSITE
USERNAME
PASSWORD
PIN/HINT
OTHER

WEBSITE
USERNAME
PASSWORD
PIN/HINT
OTHER

WEBSITE
USERNAME
PASSWORD
PIN/HINT
OTHER

WEBSITE
USERNAME
PASSWORD
PIN/HINT
OTHER

K

WEBSITE
USERNAME
PASSWORD
PIN/HINT
OTHER

WEBSITE
USERNAME
PASSWORD
PIN/HINT
OTHER

WEBSITE
USERNAME
PASSWORD
PIN/HINT
OTHER

WEBSITE
USERNAME
PASSWORD
PIN/HINT
OTHER

K

WEBSITE	
USERNAME	
PASSWORD	
PIN/HINT	
OTHER	

WEBSITE	
USERNAME	
PASSWORD	
PIN/HINT	
OTHER	

WEBSITE	
USERNAME	
PASSWORD	
PIN/HINT	
OTHER	

WEBSITE	
USERNAME	
PASSWORD	
PIN/HINT	
OTHER	

K

WEBSITE
USERNAME
PASSWORD
PIN/HINT
OTHER

WEBSITE
USERNAME
PASSWORD
PIN/HINT
OTHER

WEBSITE
USERNAME
PASSWORD
PIN/HINT
OTHER

WEBSITE
USERNAME
PASSWORD
PIN/HINT
OTHER

L

WEBSITE
USERNAME
PASSWORD
PIN/HINT
OTHER

WEBSITE
USERNAME
PASSWORD
PIN/HINT
OTHER

WEBSITE
USERNAME
PASSWORD
PIN/HINT
OTHER

WEBSITE
USERNAME
PASSWORD
PIN/HINT
OTHER

L

WEBSITE
USERNAME
PASSWORD
PIN/HINT
OTHER

WEBSITE
USERNAME
PASSWORD
PIN/HINT
OTHER

WEBSITE
USERNAME
PASSWORD
PIN/HINT
OTHER

WEBSITE
USERNAME
PASSWORD
PIN/HINT
OTHER

L

WEBSITE	
USERNAME	
PASSWORD	
PIN/HINT	
OTHER	

WEBSITE	
USERNAME	
PASSWORD	
PIN/HINT	
OTHER	

WEBSITE	
USERNAME	
PASSWORD	
PIN/HINT	
OTHER	

WEBSITE	
USERNAME	
PASSWORD	
PIN/HINT	
OTHER	

L

WEBSITE
USERNAME
PASSWORD
PIN/HINT
OTHER

WEBSITE
USERNAME
PASSWORD
PIN/HINT
OTHER

WEBSITE
USERNAME
PASSWORD
PIN/HINT
OTHER

WEBSITE
USERNAME
PASSWORD
PIN/HINT
OTHER

M

WEBSITE
USERNAME
PASSWORD
PIN/HINT
OTHER

WEBSITE
USERNAME
PASSWORD
PIN/HINT
OTHER

WEBSITE
USERNAME
PASSWORD
PIN/HINT
OTHER

WEBSITE
USERNAME
PASSWORD
PIN/HINT
OTHER

WEBSITE
USERNAME
PASSWORD
PIN/HINT
OTHER

WEBSITE
USERNAME
PASSWORD
PIN/HINT
OTHER

WEBSITE
USERNAME
PASSWORD
PIN/HINT
OTHER

WEBSITE
USERNAME
PASSWORD
PIN/HINT
OTHER

M

WEBSITE
USERNAME
PASSWORD
PIN/HINT
OTHER

WEBSITE
USERNAME
PASSWORD
PIN/HINT
OTHER

WEBSITE
USERNAME
PASSWORD
PIN/HINT
OTHER

WEBSITE
USERNAME
PASSWORD
PIN/HINT
OTHER

WEBSITE	
USERNAME	
PASSWORD	
PIN/HINT	
OTHER	

WEBSITE	
USERNAME	
PASSWORD	
PIN/HINT	
OTHER	

WEBSITE	
USERNAME	
PASSWORD	
PIN/HINT	
OTHER	

WEBSITE	
USERNAME	
PASSWORD	
PIN/HINT	
OTHER	

M

N

WEBSITE
USERNAME
PASSWORD
PIN/HINT
OTHER

WEBSITE
USERNAME
PASSWORD
PIN/HINT
OTHER

WEBSITE
USERNAME
PASSWORD
PIN/HINT
OTHER

WEBSITE
USERNAME
PASSWORD
PIN/HINT
OTHER

N

WEBSITE
USERNAME
PASSWORD
PIN/HINT
OTHER

WEBSITE
USERNAME
PASSWORD
PIN/HINT
OTHER

WEBSITE
USERNAME
PASSWORD
PIN/HINT
OTHER

WEBSITE
USERNAME
PASSWORD
PIN/HINT
OTHER

N

WEBSITE
USERNAME
PASSWORD
PIN/HINT
OTHER

WEBSITE
USERNAME
PASSWORD
PIN/HINT
OTHER

WEBSITE
USERNAME
PASSWORD
PIN/HINT
OTHER

WEBSITE
USERNAME
PASSWORD
PIN/HINT
OTHER

N

WEBSITE
USERNAME
PASSWORD
PIN/HINT
OTHER

WEBSITE
USERNAME
PASSWORD
PIN/HINT
OTHER

WEBSITE
USERNAME
PASSWORD
PIN/HINT
OTHER

WEBSITE
USERNAME
PASSWORD
PIN/HINT
OTHER

0

WEBSITE
USERNAME
PASSWORD
PIN/HINT
OTHER

WEBSITE
USERNAME
PASSWORD
PIN/HINT
OTHER

WEBSITE
USERNAME
PASSWORD
PIN/HINT
OTHER

WEBSITE
USERNAME
PASSWORD
PIN/HINT
OTHER

0

WEBSITE
USERNAME
PASSWORD
PIN/HINT
OTHER

WEBSITE
USERNAME
PASSWORD
PIN/HINT
OTHER

WEBSITE
USERNAME
PASSWORD
PIN/HINT
OTHER

WEBSITE
USERNAME
PASSWORD
PIN/HINT
OTHER

0

WEBSITE
USERNAME
PASSWORD
PIN/HINT
OTHER

WEBSITE
USERNAME
PASSWORD
PIN/HINT
OTHER

WEBSITE
USERNAME
PASSWORD
PIN/HINT
OTHER

WEBSITE
USERNAME
PASSWORD
PIN/HINT
OTHER

0

- WEBSITE
- USERNAME
- PASSWORD
- PIN/HINT
- OTHER

- WEBSITE
- USERNAME
- PASSWORD
- PIN/HINT
- OTHER

- WEBSITE
- USERNAME
- PASSWORD
- PIN/HINT
- OTHER

- WEBSITE
- USERNAME
- PASSWORD
- PIN/HINT
- OTHER

P

WEBSITE
USERNAME
PASSWORD
PIN/HINT
OTHER

WEBSITE
USERNAME
PASSWORD
PIN/HINT
OTHER

WEBSITE
USERNAME
PASSWORD
PIN/HINT
OTHER

WEBSITE
USERNAME
PASSWORD
PIN/HINT
OTHER

P

WEBSITE
USERNAME
PASSWORD
PIN/HINT
OTHER

WEBSITE
USERNAME
PASSWORD
PIN/HINT
OTHER

WEBSITE
USERNAME
PASSWORD
PIN/HINT
OTHER

WEBSITE
USERNAME
PASSWORD
PIN/HINT
OTHER

P

WEBSITE
USERNAME
PASSWORD
PIN/HINT
OTHER

WEBSITE
USERNAME
PASSWORD
PIN/HINT
OTHER

WEBSITE
USERNAME
PASSWORD
PIN/HINT
OTHER

WEBSITE
USERNAME
PASSWORD
PIN/HINT
OTHER

P

WEBSITE
USERNAME
PASSWORD
PIN/HINT
OTHER

WEBSITE
USERNAME
PASSWORD
PIN/HINT
OTHER

WEBSITE
USERNAME
PASSWORD
PIN/HINT
OTHER

WEBSITE
USERNAME
PASSWORD
PIN/HINT
OTHER

Q

WEBSITE
USERNAME
PASSWORD
PIN/HINT
OTHER

WEBSITE
USERNAME
PASSWORD
PIN/HINT
OTHER

WEBSITE
USERNAME
PASSWORD
PIN/HINT
OTHER

WEBSITE
USERNAME
PASSWORD
PIN/HINT
OTHER

Q

WEBSITE
USERNAME
PASSWORD
PIN/HINT
OTHER

WEBSITE
USERNAME
PASSWORD
PIN/HINT
OTHER

WEBSITE
USERNAME
PASSWORD
PIN/HINT
OTHER

WEBSITE
USERNAME
PASSWORD
PIN/HINT
OTHER

Q

WEBSITE	
USERNAME	
PASSWORD	
PIN/HINT	
OTHER	

WEBSITE	
USERNAME	
PASSWORD	
PIN/HINT	
OTHER	

WEBSITE	
USERNAME	
PASSWORD	
PIN/HINT	
OTHER	

WEBSITE	
USERNAME	
PASSWORD	
PIN/HINT	
OTHER	

Q

WEBSITE
USERNAME
PASSWORD
PIN/HINT
OTHER

WEBSITE
USERNAME
PASSWORD
PIN/HINT
OTHER

WEBSITE
USERNAME
PASSWORD
PIN/HINT
OTHER

WEBSITE
USERNAME
PASSWORD
PIN/HINT
OTHER

R

- WEBSITE
- USERNAME
- PASSWORD
- PIN/HINT
- OTHER

- WEBSITE
- USERNAME
- PASSWORD
- PIN/HINT
- OTHER

- WEBSITE
- USERNAME
- PASSWORD
- PIN/HINT
- OTHER

- WEBSITE
- USERNAME
- PASSWORD
- PIN/HINT
- OTHER

R

WEBSITE
USERNAME
PASSWORD
PIN/HINT
OTHER

WEBSITE
USERNAME
PASSWORD
PIN/HINT
OTHER

WEBSITE
USERNAME
PASSWORD
PIN/HINT
OTHER

WEBSITE
USERNAME
PASSWORD
PIN/HINT
OTHER

R

WEBSITE
USERNAME
PASSWORD
PIN/HINT
OTHER

WEBSITE
USERNAME
PASSWORD
PIN/HINT
OTHER

WEBSITE
USERNAME
PASSWORD
PIN/HINT
OTHER

WEBSITE
USERNAME
PASSWORD
PIN/HINT
OTHER

R

WEBSITE	
USERNAME	
PASSWORD	
PIN/HINT	
OTHER	

WEBSITE	
USERNAME	
PASSWORD	
PIN/HINT	
OTHER	

WEBSITE	
USERNAME	
PASSWORD	
PIN/HINT	
OTHER	

WEBSITE	
USERNAME	
PASSWORD	
PIN/HINT	
OTHER	

S

WEBSITE

USERNAME

PASSWORD

PIN/HINT

OTHER

WEBSITE

USERNAME

PASSWORD

PIN/HINT

OTHER

WEBSITE

USERNAME

PASSWORD

PIN/HINT

OTHER

WEBSITE

USERNAME

PASSWORD

PIN/HINT

OTHER

S

WEBSITE	
USERNAME	
PASSWORD	
PIN/HINT	
OTHER	

WEBSITE	
USERNAME	
PASSWORD	
PIN/HINT	
OTHER	

WEBSITE	
USERNAME	
PASSWORD	
PIN/HINT	
OTHER	

WEBSITE	
USERNAME	
PASSWORD	
PIN/HINT	
OTHER	

S

WEBSITE
USERNAME
PASSWORD
PIN/HINT
OTHER

WEBSITE
USERNAME
PASSWORD
PIN/HINT
OTHER

WEBSITE
USERNAME
PASSWORD
PIN/HINT
OTHER

WEBSITE
USERNAME
PASSWORD
PIN/HINT
OTHER

WEBSITE	
USERNAME	
PASSWORD	
PIN/HINT	
OTHER	

S

WEBSITE	
USERNAME	
PASSWORD	
PIN/HINT	
OTHER	

WEBSITE	
USERNAME	
PASSWORD	
PIN/HINT	
OTHER	

WEBSITE	
USERNAME	
PASSWORD	
PIN/HINT	
OTHER	

T

WEBSITE	
USERNAME	
PASSWORD	
PIN/HINT	
OTHER	

WEBSITE	
USERNAME	
PASSWORD	
PIN/HINT	
OTHER	

WEBSITE	
USERNAME	
PASSWORD	
PIN/HINT	
OTHER	

WEBSITE	
USERNAME	
PASSWORD	
PIN/HINT	
OTHER	

T

WEBSITE	
USERNAME	
PASSWORD	
PIN/HINT	
OTHER	

WEBSITE	
USERNAME	
PASSWORD	
PIN/HINT	
OTHER	

WEBSITE	
USERNAME	
PASSWORD	
PIN/HINT	
OTHER	

WEBSITE	
USERNAME	
PASSWORD	
PIN/HINT	
OTHER	

T

WEBSITE	
USERNAME	
PASSWORD	
PIN/HINT	
OTHER	

WEBSITE	
USERNAME	
PASSWORD	
PIN/HINT	
OTHER	

WEBSITE	
USERNAME	
PASSWORD	
PIN/HINT	
OTHER	

WEBSITE	
USERNAME	
PASSWORD	
PIN/HINT	
OTHER	

T

WEBSITE	
USERNAME	
PASSWORD	
PIN/HINT	
OTHER	

WEBSITE	
USERNAME	
PASSWORD	
PIN/HINT	
OTHER	

WEBSITE	
USERNAME	
PASSWORD	
PIN/HINT	
OTHER	

WEBSITE	
USERNAME	
PASSWORD	
PIN/HINT	
OTHER	

U

WEBSITE	
USERNAME	
PASSWORD	
PIN/HINT	
OTHER	

WEBSITE	
USERNAME	
PASSWORD	
PIN/HINT	
OTHER	

WEBSITE	
USERNAME	
PASSWORD	
PIN/HINT	
OTHER	

WEBSITE	
USERNAME	
PASSWORD	
PIN/HINT	
OTHER	

U

WEBSITE
USERNAME
PASSWORD
PIN/HINT
OTHER

WEBSITE
USERNAME
PASSWORD
PIN/HINT
OTHER

WEBSITE
USERNAME
PASSWORD
PIN/HINT
OTHER

WEBSITE
USERNAME
PASSWORD
PIN/HINT
OTHER

U

WEBSITE

USERNAME

PASSWORD

PIN/HINT

OTHER

WEBSITE

USERNAME

PASSWORD

PIN/HINT

OTHER

WEBSITE

USERNAME

PASSWORD

PIN/HINT

OTHER

WEBSITE

USERNAME

PASSWORD

PIN/HINT

OTHER

U

WEBSITE
USERNAME
PASSWORD
PIN/HINT
OTHER

WEBSITE
USERNAME
PASSWORD
PIN/HINT
OTHER

WEBSITE
USERNAME
PASSWORD
PIN/HINT
OTHER

WEBSITE
USERNAME
PASSWORD
PIN/HINT
OTHER

V

WEBSITE
USERNAME
PASSWORD
PIN/HINT
OTHER

WEBSITE
USERNAME
PASSWORD
PIN/HINT
OTHER

WEBSITE
USERNAME
PASSWORD
PIN/HINT
OTHER

WEBSITE
USERNAME
PASSWORD
PIN/HINT
OTHER

V

WEBSITE
USERNAME
PASSWORD
PIN/HINT
OTHER

WEBSITE
USERNAME
PASSWORD
PIN/HINT
OTHER

WEBSITE
USERNAME
PASSWORD
PIN/HINT
OTHER

WEBSITE
USERNAME
PASSWORD
PIN/HINT
OTHER

V

- WEBSITE
- USERNAME
- PASSWORD
- PIN/HINT
- OTHER

- WEBSITE
- USERNAME
- PASSWORD
- PIN/HINT
- OTHER

- WEBSITE
- USERNAME
- PASSWORD
- PIN/HINT
- OTHER

- WEBSITE
- USERNAME
- PASSWORD
- PIN/HINT
- OTHER

WEBSITE	
USERNAME	
PASSWORD	
PIN/HINT	
OTHER	

WEBSITE	
USERNAME	
PASSWORD	
PIN/HINT	
OTHER	

WEBSITE	
USERNAME	
PASSWORD	
PIN/HINT	
OTHER	

WEBSITE	
USERNAME	
PASSWORD	
PIN/HINT	
OTHER	

W

WEBSITE
USERNAME
PASSWORD
PIN/HINT
OTHER

WEBSITE
USERNAME
PASSWORD
PIN/HINT
OTHER

WEBSITE
USERNAME
PASSWORD
PIN/HINT
OTHER

WEBSITE
USERNAME
PASSWORD
PIN/HINT
OTHER

WEBSITE	
USERNAME	
PASSWORD	
PIN/HINT	
OTHER	

W

WEBSITE	
USERNAME	
PASSWORD	
PIN/HINT	
OTHER	

WEBSITE	
USERNAME	
PASSWORD	
PIN/HINT	
OTHER	

WEBSITE	
USERNAME	
PASSWORD	
PIN/HINT	
OTHER	

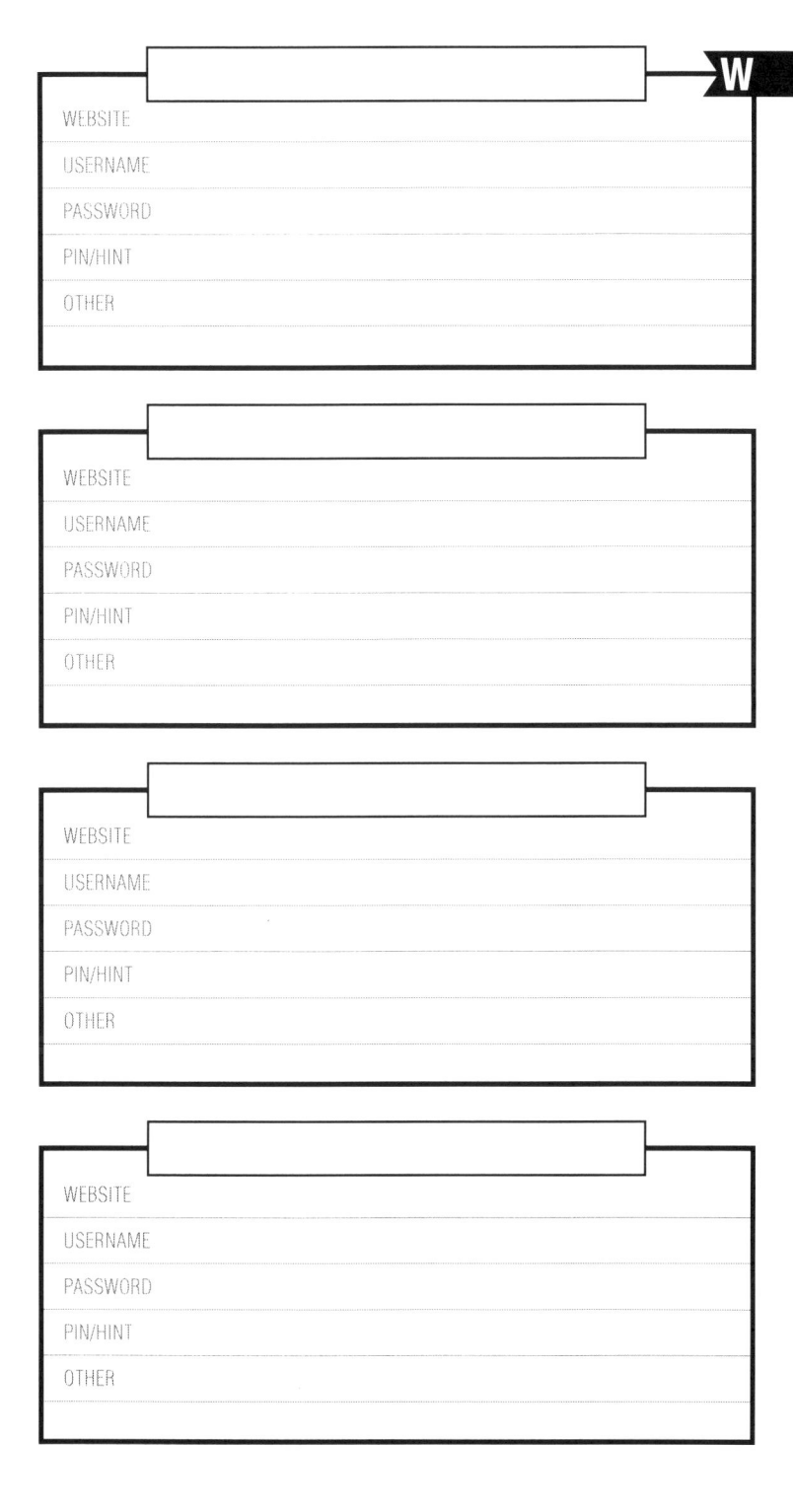

W

WEBSITE
USERNAME
PASSWORD
PIN/HINT
OTHER

WEBSITE
USERNAME
PASSWORD
PIN/HINT
OTHER

WEBSITE
USERNAME
PASSWORD
PIN/HINT
OTHER

WEBSITE
USERNAME
PASSWORD
PIN/HINT
OTHER

WEBSITE
USERNAME
PASSWORD
PIN/HINT
OTHER

WEBSITE
USERNAME
PASSWORD
PIN/HINT
OTHER

WEBSITE
USERNAME
PASSWORD
PIN/HINT
OTHER

WEBSITE
USERNAME
PASSWORD
PIN/HINT
OTHER

X

WEBSITE	
USERNAME	
PASSWORD	
PIN/HINT	
OTHER	

WEBSITE	
USERNAME	
PASSWORD	
PIN/HINT	
OTHER	

WEBSITE	
USERNAME	
PASSWORD	
PIN/HINT	
OTHER	

WEBSITE	
USERNAME	
PASSWORD	
PIN/HINT	
OTHER	

WEBSITE	
USERNAME	
PASSWORD	
PIN/HINT	
OTHER	

WEBSITE	
USERNAME	
PASSWORD	
PIN/HINT	
OTHER	

WEBSITE	
USERNAME	
PASSWORD	
PIN/HINT	
OTHER	

WEBSITE	
USERNAME	
PASSWORD	
PIN/HINT	
OTHER	

X

WEBSITE
USERNAME
PASSWORD
PIN/HINT
OTHER

WEBSITE
USERNAME
PASSWORD
PIN/HINT
OTHER

WEBSITE
USERNAME
PASSWORD
PIN/HINT
OTHER

WEBSITE
USERNAME
PASSWORD
PIN/HINT
OTHER

WEBSITE	
USERNAME	
PASSWORD	
PIN/HINT	
OTHER	

WEBSITE	
USERNAME	
PASSWORD	
PIN/HINT	
OTHER	

WEBSITE	
USERNAME	
PASSWORD	
PIN/HINT	
OTHER	

WEBSITE	
USERNAME	
PASSWORD	
PIN/HINT	
OTHER	

Y

WEBSITE
USERNAME
PASSWORD
PIN/HINT
OTHER

WEBSITE
USERNAME
PASSWORD
PIN/HINT
OTHER

WEBSITE
USERNAME
PASSWORD
PIN/HINT
OTHER

WEBSITE
USERNAME
PASSWORD
PIN/HINT
OTHER

WEBSITE	
USERNAME	
PASSWORD	
PIN/HINT	
OTHER	

Y

WEBSITE	
USERNAME	
PASSWORD	
PIN/HINT	
OTHER	

WEBSITE	
USERNAME	
PASSWORD	
PIN/HINT	
OTHER	

WEBSITE	
USERNAME	
PASSWORD	
PIN/HINT	
OTHER	

Y

WEBSITE	
USERNAME	
PASSWORD	
PIN/HINT	
OTHER	

WEBSITE	
USERNAME	
PASSWORD	
PIN/HINT	
OTHER	

WEBSITE	
USERNAME	
PASSWORD	
PIN/HINT	
OTHER	

WEBSITE	
USERNAME	
PASSWORD	
PIN/HINT	
OTHER	

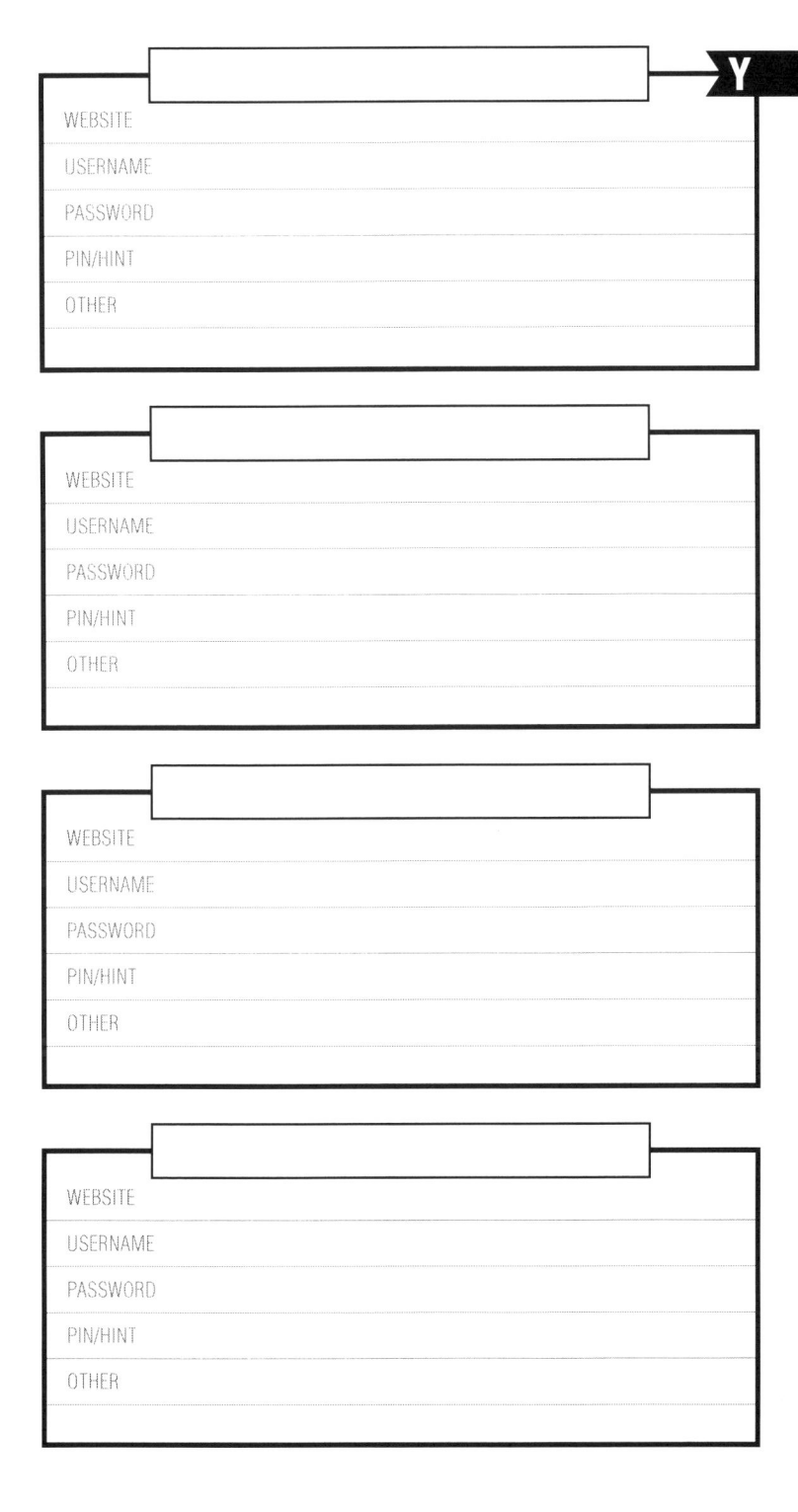

Y

WEBSITE
USERNAME
PASSWORD
PIN/HINT
OTHER

WEBSITE
USERNAME
PASSWORD
PIN/HINT
OTHER

WEBSITE
USERNAME
PASSWORD
PIN/HINT
OTHER

WEBSITE
USERNAME
PASSWORD
PIN/HINT
OTHER

Z

WEBSITE

USERNAME

PASSWORD

PIN/HINT

OTHER

WEBSITE

USERNAME

PASSWORD

PIN/HINT

OTHER

WEBSITE

USERNAME

PASSWORD

PIN/HINT

OTHER

WEBSITE

USERNAME

PASSWORD

PIN/HINT

OTHER

Z

WEBSITE	
USERNAME	
PASSWORD	
PIN/HINT	
OTHER	

WEBSITE	
USERNAME	
PASSWORD	
PIN/HINT	
OTHER	

WEBSITE	
USERNAME	
PASSWORD	
PIN/HINT	
OTHER	

WEBSITE	
USERNAME	
PASSWORD	
PIN/HINT	
OTHER	

Z

WEBSITE
USERNAME
PASSWORD
PIN/HINT
OTHER

WEBSITE
USERNAME
PASSWORD
PIN/HINT
OTHER

WEBSITE
USERNAME
PASSWORD
PIN/HINT
OTHER

WEBSITE
USERNAME
PASSWORD
PIN/HINT
OTHER

Z

WEBSITE
USERNAME
PASSWORD
PIN/HINT
OTHER

WEBSITE
USERNAME
PASSWORD
PIN/HINT
OTHER

WEBSITE
USERNAME
PASSWORD
PIN/HINT
OTHER

WEBSITE
USERNAME
PASSWORD
PIN/HINT
OTHER

Manufactured by Amazon.ca
Bolton, ON